INTERNATIONAL CENTRE FOR MECHANICAL SCIENCES

COURSES AND LECTURES - No. 109

GIUSEPPE BASILE
UNIVERSITY OF GENOVA

CONTROLLED AND CONDITIONED INVARIANCE

COURSE HELD AT THE DEPARTMENT
OF AUTOMATION AND INFORMATION
JULY 1971

UDINE 1971

SPRINGER-VERLAG WIEN GMBH

This work is subject to copyright.

All rights are reserved,

whether the whole or part of the material is concerned

specifically those of translation, reprinting, re-use of illustrations,

broadcasting, reproduction by photocopying machine

or similar means, and storage in data banks.

© 1972 by Springer-Verlag Wien

Originally published by Springer-Verlag Wien-New York in 1972

ISBN 978-3-211-81132-0   ISBN 978-3-7091-2953-1 (eBook)
DOI 10.1007/978-3-7091-2953-1

FOREWORD

The present course on the "Controlled and Conditioned Invariance" is devoted to familiarizing people, who are someway interested in control problems, with the mathematical tools which are the basis of structural analysis.

In order to give clear pictures which illustrate the topological aspects of the problems, the completeness and the mathematical rigor in some points have been sacrificed. In so doing, the methodology characteristic of this type of analysis comes out clearly and the reader gets a complete idea of the problems which can be efficiently approached by means of structural analysis.

The author is very grateful to CISM and, in particular to the General Secretary, professor Luigi Sobrero, for giving him the opportunity of delivering this course.

Introduction

We consider in the present paper the analysis of linear time-invariant dynamic systems. The analysis will be carried out from a structural viewpoint: in other words, looking at the structure of the system (geometric properties of the linear transformations represented by its matrices) some important aspects of its behaviour will be investigated.

Among those properties which are interesing in control problems, the controllability will be completely analyzed here.

In part One the generalization of the concept of invariance of a subspace under a linear transforamtion will be presented. In Part Two the mathematical tools provided in Part One will be applied to the analysis of the controllability.

Some linear algebraic background is reported for the reader's convenience in the Appendix at the end of Part One.

Part one

GENERALIZATION OF THE CONCEPT OF INVARIANCE

1.1. The simple invariance

Given in $\mathcal{R}^n$ a linear transformation represented by the square constant matrix A, and a linear subspace $\mathcal{J} \subset \mathcal{R}^n$, $\mathcal{J}$ is an A-invariant if

(1.1.1) $$A\mathcal{J} \subseteq \mathcal{J};$$

$A\mathcal{J}$ clearly idicates the transformed of $\mathcal{J}$ in the linear transformation A.

Of course the origin and the full space $\mathcal{R}^n$ are invariants under every linear transformation.

By

$$mi(A, \mathcal{X})$$

in the following will be indicated the minimum A-invariant containing the subspace $\mathcal{X}$, and by

$$MI(A, \mathcal{X})$$

the maximum A-invariant contained in $\mathcal{X}$.

In Section 1.5 the algorithms for the computation of $mi(A, \mathcal{X})$ and $MI(A, \mathcal{X})$ will be given.

Controlled and conditioned invariance

1.2. The controlled invariance

Given in $\mathcal{R}^n$ the linear transformation A and the "controlling" subspace $\mathcal{F}$, a subspace $\hat{\mathcal{J}}$ is a <u>controlled invariant under A with respect to $\mathcal{F}$</u>, or simply an <u>$(A,\mathcal{F})$-controlled invariant</u>, if

$$A\hat{\mathcal{J}} \subseteq \hat{\mathcal{J}} + \mathcal{F} . \qquad (1.2.2)$$

Of course every simple invariant under A is a controlled invariant with respect to any $\mathcal{F}$, and in particular with respect to $\mathcal{F} = 0$.

- If $\mathcal{F} = \mathcal{R}^n$, relationship (1.2.2) is verified by every subspace and every matrix.
- The origin and the full space are controlled invariants under every matrix with respect to any $\mathcal{F}$.
- The sum of two $(A,\mathcal{F})$-controlled invariants is still an $(A,\mathcal{F})$--controlled invariant.

By

$$MCI(A, \mathcal{F}, \mathcal{X})$$

will be indicated the maximum $(A,\mathcal{F})$-controlled invariant contained in $\mathcal{X}$. If $\mathcal{F} = 0$

$$MCI(A, \mathcal{F}, \mathcal{X}) = MI(A, \mathcal{X}) . \qquad (1.2.3)$$

1.3. The conditioned invariance

Given in $\mathcal{R}^n$ the linear transformation A and the "conditioning" subspace $\mathcal{F}$, a subspace $\check{\mathcal{J}}$ is a <u>conditioned invariant under A with respect to $\mathcal{F}$</u>, or simply an <u>(A, $\mathcal{F}$)-conditioned invariant</u>, if

$$(1.3.4) \qquad A(\check{\mathcal{J}} \cap \mathcal{F}) \subseteq \check{\mathcal{J}}.$$

- Every simple A-invariant is a conditioned invariant in A with respect to any $\mathcal{F}$, and in particular with respect to $\mathcal{F} = \mathcal{R}^n$.
- If $\mathcal{F} = 0$, (1.3.4) is verified by every subspace and every matrix.
- The origin and the full space are conditioned invariants for every A and $\mathcal{F}$.
- The intersection of two $(A, \mathcal{F})$-conditioned invariants is still an $(A, \mathcal{F})$-conditioned invariant.

By

$$mci(A, \mathcal{F}, \mathcal{X})$$

will be indicated the minimum $(A, \mathcal{F})$-conditioned invariant containing $\mathcal{X}$. If $\mathcal{F} = \mathcal{R}^n$

$$(1.3.5) \qquad mci(A, \mathcal{F}, \mathcal{X}) = mi(A, \mathcal{X}).$$

1.4. A fundamental duality property

In the present section will be proved the follow-

Controlled and conditioned invariance

ing theorem which states an important duality between controlled and conditioned invariants.

THEOREM 1.1.

Given in $\mathcal{R}^n$ the linear transformation A and the subspaces $\mathcal{F}$ and $\mathcal{X}$, the orthogonal complement of $mci(A, \mathcal{F}, \mathcal{X})$ is the $MCI(A^T, \mathcal{F}^\perp, \mathcal{X}^\perp)$.

First of all it will be shown that the orthogonal complement of any $(A, \mathcal{F})$-conditioned invariant is an $(A^T, \mathcal{F}^\perp)$-controlled invariant and vice-versa.

In fact, from

$$A(\check{\mathcal{J}} \cap \mathcal{F}) \subseteq \check{\mathcal{J}} , \qquad (1.4.6)$$

applying the well-known relationship

$$\mathcal{Y} \supseteq A\mathcal{X} \rightleftarrows A^T \mathcal{Y}^\perp \subseteq \mathcal{X}^\perp , \qquad (1.4.7)$$

it comes out

$$A^T \check{\mathcal{J}}^\perp \subseteq (\check{\mathcal{J}} \cap \mathcal{F})^\perp ; \qquad (1.4.8)$$

and, using the identity

$$(\mathcal{X}_1 \cap \mathcal{X}_2)^\perp = \mathcal{X}_1^\perp + \mathcal{X}_2^\perp \qquad (1.4.9)$$

(1.4.8) gives immediately

$$A^T \check{\mathcal{J}}^\perp \subseteq \check{\mathcal{J}}^\perp + \mathcal{F}^\perp , \qquad (1.4.10)$$

which shows that $\check{\mathcal{J}}^\perp$ is an $(A^T, \mathcal{F}^\perp)$-controlled invariant. Similarly, starting from the definition of an $(A, \mathcal{F})$-controlled invariant,

(1.4.11) $$A\hat{\mathcal{J}} \subseteq \hat{\mathcal{J}} + \mathcal{F}$$

and using (1.4.7) and (1.4.9), the vice-versa can be easily proved.

It has still to be proved that $(mci(A,\mathcal{F},\mathcal{X}))^\perp$ is the maximum $(A^T, \mathcal{F}^\perp)$-controlled invariant contained in $\mathcal{X}^\perp$. Reasoning by contradiction call

(1.4.12) $$\mathcal{J} = (mci(A, \mathcal{F}, \mathcal{X}))^\perp$$

and assume $\mathcal{J}$ is not the maximum $(A^T, \mathcal{F}^\perp)$-controlled invariant contained in $\mathcal{X}^\perp$; then, calling $MCI(A^T, \mathcal{F}^\perp, \mathcal{X}^\perp)$ such a maximum:

(1.4.13) $$\mathcal{J} \subseteq MCI(A^T, \mathcal{F}^\perp, \mathcal{X}^\perp)$$

Taking the orthogonal complement of both sides of (1.4.13) it results

(1.4.14) $$\mathcal{J}^\perp \supseteq (MCI(A^T, \mathcal{F}^\perp, \mathcal{X}^\perp))^\perp \supseteq \mathcal{X}$$

But, because of its definition $\mathcal{J}^\perp$ is the minimum $(A, \mathcal{F})$-conditioned invariant containing $\mathcal{X}$ and it cannot contain any other $(A, \mathcal{F})$-conditioned invariant containing $\mathcal{X}$ like $(MCI(A^T, \mathcal{F}^\perp, \mathcal{X}^\perp))^\perp$. Then (1.4.13) holds with the equality sign.

1.5. Computational procedures for the controlled and conditioned invariants

This computation of the maximum $(A, \mathcal{F})$-controlled invariant contained in a given s.s. $\mathcal{X}$, i.e the $MCI(A, \mathcal{F}, \mathcal{X})$, may be carried out by means of the following sequence of subspaces:

$$\mathcal{Z}_0 = \mathcal{X}$$
$$\mathcal{Z}_1 = \mathcal{Z}_0 \cap A^{-1*}(\mathcal{Z}_0 + \mathcal{F})$$
$$\text{---------} \qquad (1.5.15)$$
$$\mathcal{Z}_k = \mathcal{Z}_{k-1} \cap A^{-1*}(\mathcal{Z}_{k-1} + \mathcal{F})$$

where $A^{-1*}S$ is the s.s. of all points mapped into S by the l.t. A (See in the Appendix the remarks on the pseudoinverse).

The above presented sequence is a sequence of non increasing-dimensional subspaces all contained in $\mathcal{X}$; if for some r

$$\mathcal{Z}_r = \mathcal{Z}_{r-1} \qquad (1.5.16)$$

$\mathcal{Z}_r$ is a controlled invariant contained in $\mathcal{X}$.

In fact (1.5.16) implies that

$$A^{-1*}(\mathcal{Z}_{r-1} + \mathcal{F}) \supseteq \mathcal{Z}_{r-1} \qquad (1.5.17)$$

and transforming both sides by A

$$A\mathcal{Z}_{r-1} \subseteq \mathcal{Z}_{r-1} + \mathcal{F}. \qquad (1.5.18)$$

When (1.5.16) is verified

$$Z_r = Z_{r+1} = Z_{r+2} = \ldots ;$$

and, because the sequence at most stops in $n-1$ steps, the equality

(1.5.19) $\qquad Z_n = Z_{n-1}$

holds in any case.

By contradiction finally it can be easily proved that Z_{n-1} is the maximum $(A, \mathcal{F})$-controlled invariant contained in $\mathcal{X}$.

In fact let there exist a subspace $\mathcal{J}$ such that

a) $\qquad A\mathcal{J} \subseteq \mathcal{J} + \mathcal{F}$

b) $\qquad \mathcal{J} \subseteq \mathcal{X}$

c) $\qquad \mathcal{J} \supseteq Z_{n-1} ;$

because of a) and b)

a') $\qquad \mathcal{J} \subseteq \mathcal{X} \cap A^{-1*}(\mathcal{J} + \mathcal{F}) = Z_1$

and

b') $\qquad A\mathcal{J} \subseteq Z_1 + \mathcal{F}$

Because of a') and b')

a'') $\mathcal{J} \subseteq Z_1 \cap A^{-1*}(Z_1 + \mathcal{F}) = Z_2 ,$

and so on.

Controlled and conditioned invariance

This procedure ends with

$$\mathcal{J} \subseteq \mathcal{Z}_{n-1} \qquad (1.5.20)$$

which, together with condition c) means

$$\mathcal{J} = \mathcal{Z}_{n-1}$$

Thus it has been proved completely that

$$MCI(A, \mathcal{F}, \mathcal{X}) = \mathcal{Z}_{n-1}$$

Letting $\mathcal{F} = 0$, sequence (1.5.15) gives the $MI(A, \mathcal{X})$.

The computation of the $mci(A, \mathcal{F}, \mathcal{X})$ can be done, in a perfectly dual way, using the following sequence of subspaces:

$$\begin{aligned} \mathcal{Y}_0 &= \mathcal{X} \\ \mathcal{Y}_1 &= \mathcal{Y}_0 + A(\mathcal{Y}_0 \cap \mathcal{F}) \\ &\text{--------} \\ \mathcal{Y}_k &= \mathcal{Y}_{k-1} + A(\mathcal{Y}_{k-1} \cap \mathcal{F}) \end{aligned} \qquad (1.5.21)$$

The terms of the sequence are subspaces of non decreasing dimensions, all containing $\mathcal{X}$, if for some r

$$\mathcal{Y}_r = \mathcal{Y}_{r-1} \qquad (1.5.22)$$

then

$$A(\mathcal{Y}_{r-1} \cap \mathcal{F}) \subseteq \mathcal{Y}_{r-1} \qquad (1.5.23)$$

which means that $\mathcal{Y}_{r-1}$ is an $(A,\mathcal{F})$-conditioned invariant.

In such a case

$$\mathcal{Y}_r = \mathcal{Y}_{r+1} \ldots,$$

and, because the sequence, at most, stops in $n-1$ steps, $\mathcal{Y}_{n-1}$ certainly coincides with $\mathcal{Y}_n$.

By contradiction again, let there exist a subspace $\mathcal{J}$ such that

a) $\quad A(\mathcal{J} \cap \mathcal{F}) \subseteq \mathcal{J}$

b) $\quad \mathcal{J} \supseteq \mathcal{X}$

c) $\quad \mathcal{J} \subseteq \mathcal{Y}_{n-1}$:

from a) and b) it follows immediately

a') $\quad \mathcal{J} \supseteq \mathcal{X} + A(\mathcal{X} \cap \mathcal{F}) = \mathcal{Y}_1$

and then

b') $\quad A(\mathcal{Y}_1 \cap \mathcal{F}) \subseteq \mathcal{J}$.

From a') and b')

a'') $\quad \mathcal{J} \supseteq \mathcal{Y}_1 + A(\mathcal{Y}_1 \cap \mathcal{F}) = \mathcal{Y}_2$

and so on. The procedure ends with

(1.5.24) $\quad \mathcal{J} \supseteq \mathcal{Y}_{n-1}$

(1.5.24) and condition c) can both be valid if the equality sign holds, then

$$\mathcal{J} = \mathcal{Y}_{n-1} = mci(A, \mathcal{F}, \mathcal{X}).$$

Letting $\mathcal{F} = \mathcal{R}^n$, the sequence (1.5.21) gives the expression of

$$mi(A, \mathcal{F}) = \mathcal{F} + A\mathcal{F} + \ldots + A^{n-1}\mathcal{F}. \quad (1.5.25)$$

Appendix
The pseudoinverse of a singular matrix

Let C be a nonsquare matrix with s rows and n columns mapping $\mathcal{R}^n$ into $\mathcal{R}^s$, $(s<n)$.

Denoting by $\mathcal{R}(C)$ and $\mathcal{N}(C)$ the range and the null space of C, the following well-known equalities hold:

(a.1) $\quad \mathcal{N}(C) = (\mathcal{R}(C^T))^{\perp}$ or $\mathcal{N}(C) + \mathcal{R}(C^T) = \mathcal{R}^n$,

(a.2) $\quad \mathcal{N}(C^T) = (\mathcal{R}(C))^{\perp}$ or $\mathcal{N}(C^T) + \mathcal{R}(C) = \mathcal{R}^s$.

Any vector $\underline{x} \in \mathcal{R}^n$ can be decomposed in $\underline{x}_1 \in \mathcal{R}(C^T)$ and $\underline{x}_2 \in \mathcal{N}(C)$ in a unique way: then

(a.3) $\quad\quad\quad\quad C\underline{x} = C\underline{x}_1 + C\underline{x}_2$

and, because the second term in the right side member clearly vanishes, before transforming by C, one can always project on the $\mathcal{R}(C^T)$.

Since $\mathcal{R}(C)$ and $\mathcal{R}(C^T)$ have the same dimensions, it is possible to find a 1 to 1 linear transformation mapping $\mathcal{R}(C)$ into $\mathcal{R}(C^T)$.

If V is a basis matrix for $\mathcal{R}(C)$, and U is a basis matrix for $\mathcal{R}(C^T)$, such a linear operator can be expressed as

Pseudo inverse of a singular matrix

$$\tilde{C}^{-1} = U(V^T V)^{-1} V^T \qquad (a.4)$$

$\tilde{C}^{-1}$ clearly is a square nonsingular matrix by virtue of the definition of U and V.

Given a subspace of $\mathcal{R}^s$, say S, the subspace Z of all points in $\mathcal{R}^n$, which are mapped by C into S is

$$Z = \tilde{C}^{-1} S + \mathcal{N}(C) = C^{-1*} S \qquad (a.5)$$

Of course S must belong to $\mathcal{R}(C)$: if not only the part $S \cap \mathcal{R}(C)$ can be inverted.

In this case

$$Z = \tilde{C}^{-1}(S \cap \mathcal{R}(C)) + \mathcal{N}(C)$$

is the locus of all the points mapped by C into the intersection of S with $\mathcal{R}(C)$.

References

[1] Halmos, P.R. : "Finite Dimensional Vector Spaces"
   Van Nostrand, N.Y., 1958

[2] Lanczos, C. : "Linear Differential Operators"
   Van Nostrand, London, 1961

[3] Basile, G. : "Some Remarks on the Pseudoinverse of a Non-square Matrix"
   Atti dell'Accademia delle Scienze di Bologna
   Serie XII, Tomo VI, Anno 257°, 1969

[4] Basile, G. and Marro, G. : "Controlled and Conditioned Invariant Subspaces in Linear System Theory"
   Journal of Opt. Th. and Appl. Vol. 3, N° 5, 1969

[5] Basile, G., Laschi, R. and Marro, G. : "Invarianza controllata e non-interazione nello spazio degli stati"
   L'Elettrotecnica, N° 1, 1969

Part two

CONTROLLABILITY OF LINEAR DYNAMIC SYSTEMS

2.1. Preliminary definitions

Consider the linear purely dynamic system described by the mathematical model

$$\dot{\underline{x}} = A\underline{x} + B\underline{u} \qquad (2.1.1)$$

$$\underline{y} = C\underline{x} \quad , \qquad (2.1.2)$$

where $\underline{x} \in \mathcal{R}^n$ is the state vector, $\underline{u} \in \mathcal{R}^m$ the input vector, $\underline{y} \in \mathcal{R}^s$ the output vector; A, B, C constant $n \times n$, $n \times m$ and $s \times m$ matrices.

In the following by $\mathcal{R}(B)$ will be indicated the range of matrix B, which is the subspace of the input actions.

Controllability is a property of the system (2.1.1) (2.1.2) connected with the structural properties of the linear transformations A, B and C.

The fundamental characteristics of such a property can be investigated in both state-space and output space so that one will speak in the following about state controllability and output controllability.

It is possible to give several different definitions of controllability, which have been summarized in the diagram of Fig. 1

2.2. Unconstrained state pointwise controllability

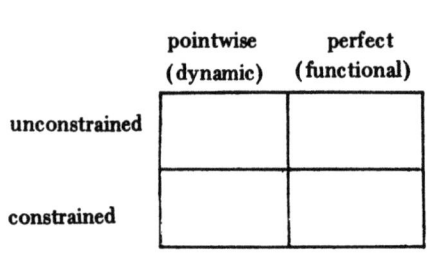

Fig. 1.

Starting from the origin of the state space it is requested to control the system in such a way as to reach a given point of $\mathcal{R}^n$, without imposing any condition on the trajectory that the system follows during its evolution.

The problem has a solution if and only if the assigned target belongs to the subspace of reachable points.

As it is well-known, such a subspace is expressed by

(2.2.3) $$\mathcal{X} = mi(A, \mathcal{R}(B))$$

The proof is immediate: first of all one can observe that the trajectory must belong entirely to $\mathcal{X}_R$, otherwise it would be possible to reach points outside $\mathcal{X}_R$, and then also the velocity $\dot{x}$ must belong to $\mathcal{X}_R$ at each point of the trajectory.

Besides this, because starting at the origin it is possible to impose to the system all velocities in $\mathcal{R}(B)$, $\mathcal{X}_R$ must contain $\mathcal{R}(B)$:

(a) $$\mathcal{X}_R \supseteq \mathcal{R}(B) .$$

State controllability

On the other hand, if at each point $\underline{x} \in \mathcal{X}_R$ every possible velocity must belong to $\mathcal{X}_R$, the following relationship has to be verified

$$A\mathcal{X}_R + \mathcal{R}(B) \subseteq \mathcal{X}_R ; \qquad (2.2.4)$$

which, taking into account a) becomes

$$A\mathcal{X}_R \subseteq \mathcal{X}_R \qquad (b)$$

a) and b) show that $\mathcal{X}_R$ is an A-invariant containing $\mathcal{R}(B)$. Clearly $\mathcal{X}_R$ is the minimum A-invariant containing $\mathcal{R}(B)$ because at each of its points it is impossible to impose to the system a velocity not belonging to $\mathcal{X}_R$. Expression (2.1.3) is so proved.

A simple example

Consider the electric network shown in Fig. 2

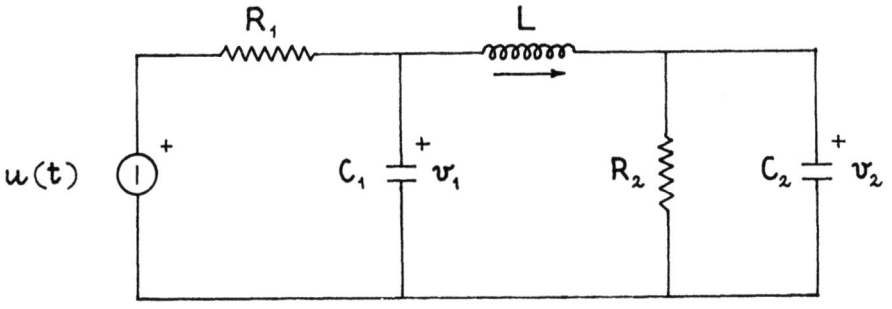

Fig. 2.

The voltages of the condensers and the current across the inductor are the state variables, the voltage of the ideal generator is the input variable.

Part Two – Controllability of linear dynamic systems

The system equations are:

$$\frac{d}{dt}\begin{vmatrix} v_1 \\ v_2 \\ i \end{vmatrix} = \begin{vmatrix} -\frac{1}{C_1 R_1} & 0 & -\frac{1}{C_1} \\ 0 & -\frac{1}{C_2 R_2} & \frac{1}{C_2} \\ \frac{1}{L} & -\frac{1}{L} & 0 \end{vmatrix} \begin{vmatrix} v_1 \\ v_2 \\ i \end{vmatrix} + \begin{vmatrix} \frac{1}{C_1 R_1} \\ 0 \\ 0 \end{vmatrix} u(t) \; ,$$

Where matrix B reduces to the only vector

$$\underline{b} = \begin{bmatrix} \frac{1}{C_1 R_1} \\ 0 \\ 0 \end{bmatrix}$$

and then $\mathcal{R}(B)$ is the first reference axis of the threedimensional state space.

$$A\underline{b} = \begin{bmatrix} -\frac{1}{C_1^2 R_1^2} \\ 0 \\ \frac{1}{L C_1 R_1} \end{bmatrix}$$

is a vector of the plane (x_1, x_3), not coincident with the first axis, and then $\underline{b} + A\underline{b}$ makes the plane (x_1, x_3).

Finally the computation of $A^2\underline{b}$ gives:

$$A^2\underline{b} = \begin{vmatrix} \frac{1}{C_1^3 R_1^3} - \frac{1}{C_1^2 L R_1} \\ \frac{1}{LC_1 C_2 R_1} \\ -\frac{1}{LC_1^2 R_1^2} \end{vmatrix}$$

being non-zero the second component, the full state space $\mathcal{R}^3$ is reachable from the origin.

The <u>not-reachable subspace</u>, or briefly the uncontrollability subspace, is the orthogonal complement of $\mathcal{X}_R$:

$$\mathcal{X}_R^\perp = \left(mi(A, \mathcal{R}(B))\right)^\perp = MI\left(A^T, (\mathcal{R}(B))^\perp\right),$$

and, observing that

$$\left(\mathcal{R}(B)\right)^\perp = \mathcal{N}(B^T) ,$$
$$\mathcal{X}_R^\perp = \mathcal{X}_U = MI\left(A^T, \mathcal{N}(B^T)\right) .$$

2.3. Constrained state pointwise controllability

The problem of the constrained controllability in the state space can be posed as follows: given a subspace $W \subseteq \mathcal{R}^n$, one wants to drive the system state in order to reach all possible points of W by means of trajectories completely belonging to W.

The problem can be approached in two different ways: first, let us find the maximum A-invariant contained in $\mathbb{W}$

(2.3.5) $\qquad \mathcal{J}_1 = MI(A, \mathbb{W})$

and assume as a set of control actions the linear subset of $\mathcal{R}(B)$ defined as

(2.3.6) $\qquad \mathcal{J}_1 \cap \mathcal{R}(B) = \mathcal{R}(G)$

where G is a constant matrix whose columns are a basis in $\mathcal{J}_1 \cap \mathcal{R}(B)$

As is well-known, in this case the subspace of all reachable points is

(2.3.7) $\qquad \mathcal{X}_{cR} = mi(A, \mathcal{R}(G))$

clearly belonging to $\mathbb{W}$ by virtue of the definition of $\mathcal{R}(G)$.

This procedure corresponds to the block diagram shown in Fig. 3

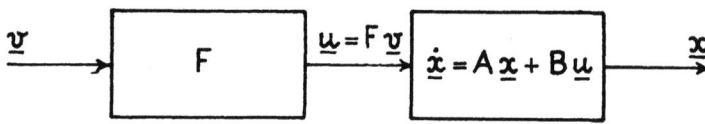

Fig. 3.

If $G = BF$ all trajectories starting at the origin of the state space belong entirely to $\mathbb{W}$ for any choice of the controls $\underline{v}$: in other words, the problem is reduced to a problem of

State controllability

unconstrained controllability limiting the control actions to $\mathcal{R}(G)$.

By doing so, the possibilities of the control have not been completely used: in fact, it is possible to reach a part of W larger than $\mathcal{X}_{cR}$, by means of a more sophisticated controller.

It is useful for this purpose the following

THEOREM 2.1.

Starting at the point $\underline{x}_0 \in W \subseteq \mathcal{R}^n$, the system can be controlled in such a way that its state trajectory lies on W for a finite interval of time, if and only if $\underline{x}_0$ belongs to the maximum $(A, \mathcal{R}(B))$ controlled invariant contained in W.

Proof.

If one calls

$$\mathcal{J}_M = MCI(A, \mathcal{R}(B), W), \quad (2.3.8)$$

it results

$$A\mathcal{J}_M \subseteq \mathcal{J}_M + \mathcal{R}(B). \quad (2.3.9)$$

By virtue of (2.3.9), the equation

$$A\underline{x} = \underline{x}' + B\underline{u}, \quad (2.3.10)$$

for every $\underline{x} \in \mathcal{J}_M$, has at least a solution $\underline{x}'$ and $\underline{u}$:

$$\underline{x}' = K_1 \underline{x} \in \mathcal{J}_M \quad (2.3.11)$$

(2.3.12) $$\underline{u} = K_2 \underline{x} \in \mathcal{R}(B)$$

where K_1 and K_2 are proper matrices.

Consider now the solution of the homogeneous differential equation

(2.3.13) $$\underline{\dot{x}} = (A - BK_2)\underline{x}$$

starting at the initial point

$$\underline{x}_0 \in \mathcal{J}_0 \ .$$

Condition (2.3.10) ensures that, for every $\underline{x} \in \mathcal{J}_M$, the velocity vector $(A - BK_2)\underline{x}$ belongs to $\mathcal{J}_M$ and then the solution of (2.3.13) entirely lies on $\mathcal{J}_M$.

Viceversa, let there exist a trajectory $\underline{x}^*(t)$ which belongs to W in the interval of time $(0, T)$. Indicating by $\mathcal{X}$ the subspace of minimal dimension which contains $\underline{x}^*(t)$, $0 \le t \le T$, (say p is its dimension), one can always choose p instants of time such that

$$\underline{x}_1 = \underline{x}^*(t_1), \ \ldots\ , \underline{x}_p = \underline{x}^*(t_p)$$

are basis vectors over $\mathcal{X}$.

In the same instants of time the velocities $\underline{\dot{x}}(t_1), \ \ldots\ , \underline{\dot{x}}(t_p)$ also belong to $\mathcal{X}$ by hypothesis, then there exist p values of the control vector such that

State controllability

$$\dot{x}_i = A x_i + B u_i \quad i = 1, \ldots, p . \qquad (2.3.14)$$

By linearly combining those last equations, it turns out

$$\sum_{k=1}^{p} a_k \dot{x}_k = A \sum_{k=1}^{p} a_k x_k + B \sum_{k=1}^{p} a_k u_k . \qquad (2.3.15)$$

Since the left-side member of (2.3.15) belongs to $\mathcal{X}$, and the vector which is transformed by A in the right-side member ranges over $\mathcal{X}$, one can conclude that, for every $x \in \mathcal{X}$ there exists a control action in $\mathcal{R}(B)$, such that the resulting velocity belongs to $\mathcal{X}$ again.

In other words

$$A \mathcal{X} \subseteq \mathcal{X} + \mathcal{R}(B)$$

Then $\mathcal{X}$ is an $(A, \mathcal{R}(B))$ controlled invariant contained in W, and therefore contained also in $\mathcal{J}_M$.

For the theory presented above, also the property stated by the following theorem is of primary importance:

THEOREM 2.2

By means of a state algebraic feedback it is possible to convert an $(A, \mathcal{R}(B))$-controlled invariant in a simple invariant.

Proof.

Call $\mathcal{X}$ the subspace of $\mathcal{R}^n$ which has to become a simple invariant for the controlled system. First of all $\mathcal{X}$ must be a $(A, \mathcal{R}(B))$ controlled invariant, otherwise it would exist at least a point $\underline{x}_0 \in \mathcal{X}$ in which it would not be possible to have a velocity on $\mathcal{X}$ for a proper control choice.

Then let p be the dimension of $\mathcal{X}$ and

$$\underline{x}_1, \ldots, \underline{x}_p \to X$$

a basis for it.

As $\mathcal{X}$ is a controlled invariant under A with respect to $\mathcal{R}(B)$, there exist $\underline{x}_1, \ldots, \underline{x}'_p \in \mathcal{X}$ and $\underline{u}_1, \ldots, \underline{u}_p \in \mathcal{R}^m$ such that

$$(2.3.16) \qquad A\underline{x}_i = \underline{x}'_i - B\underline{u}_i \qquad i = 1, \ldots, p.$$

Every point of $\mathcal{X}$ can now be expressed as a linear combination of the basis vectors:

$$(2.3.17) \quad \underline{x} = a_1 \underline{x}_1 + \ldots + a_p \underline{x}_p = X\underline{a}, \qquad \underline{a} \in \mathcal{R}^p$$

and associating to it the control obtained as a linear combination of $\underline{u}_1, \ldots, \underline{u}_p$ with the same coefficients $a_1, \ldots, a_p$ i.e

$$(2.3.18) \qquad \underline{u} = a_1 \underline{u}_1 + \ldots + a_p \underline{u}_p = U\underline{a}$$

(U is the matrix having $\underline{u}_1, \ldots, \underline{u}_p$ as columns), the resulting velocity belongs to $\mathcal{X}$.

By the choice

State controllability

$$\underline{u} = H \underline{x} \qquad (2.3.19)$$

$$H = U(X^T X)^{-1} X, \quad (*) \qquad (2.3.20)$$

condition (2.3.18) is satisfied and $\mathcal{X}$ is a simple invariant for the complete controlled system in the dotted line of Fig. 4, whose equations are
(2.3.21)

$$\underline{\dot{x}} = (A + BH)\underline{x} + B\underline{v}$$

in fact it has been shown that
(2.3.22)

$$(A + BH)\mathcal{X} \subseteq \mathcal{X}$$

under the hypothesis

$$A\mathcal{X} \subseteq \mathcal{X} + \mathcal{R}(B).$$

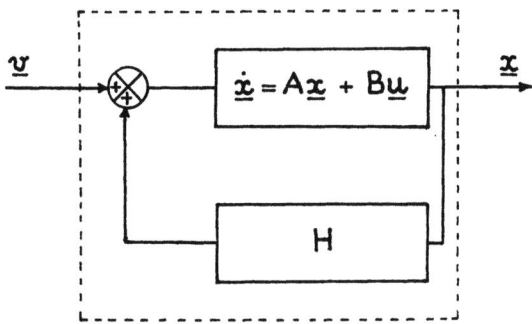

Fig. 4.

The problem of finding the largest part of a given subspace, W, reachable by means of trajectories completely lying on it, may now be promptly solved.

(+) In the choice of matrix H there is a large number of degrees of freedom. In fact, the vectors of the basis on $\mathcal{X}$, $\underline{x}_1, \ldots, \underline{x}_p$, may be chosen in a complete free way, provided, of course, they are linearly independent.

If one limits the choice of the controls to the subspace

(2.3.23) $$\mathcal{J}_M \cap \mathcal{R}(B) = \mathcal{R}(G_1)$$

any state trajectory of the controlled system shown in Fig. 4, starting at the origin, cannot leave the subspace $\mathcal{J} \subseteq W$, and so the constraint is satisfied; the reachable set in this case is

(2.3.24) $$\widetilde{\mathcal{X}}_{cR} = mi(A + BH, \mathcal{R}(G_1))$$

Clearly, $\widetilde{\mathcal{X}}_{cR}$ is larger than $\mathcal{X}_{cR}$ given by expression (2.3.7).

Again, if F_1 is such a matrix that

(2.3.25) $$G_1 = B F_1$$

the system can be controlled according to the block diagram of Fig. 5.

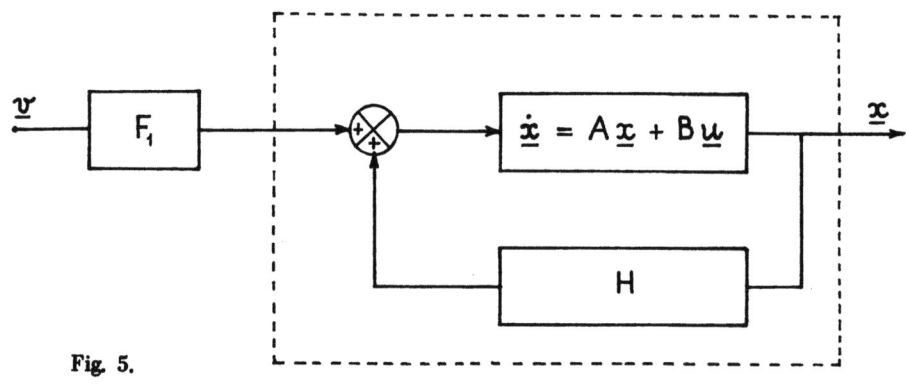

Fig. 5.

State controllability

The result expressed by relationship (2.3.24) is not complete until it has been proved that the subspace $\widetilde{X}_{cR}$ does not depend on the particular choice of the feedback matrix H. In other words, let H_1 and H_2 be two matrices such that

$$(A + BH_1)\mathcal{J}_M \subseteq \mathcal{J}_M \qquad (2.3.26)$$

$$(A + BH_2)\mathcal{J}_M \subseteq \mathcal{J}_M \qquad (2.3.27)$$

it must be proved that

$$mi(A + BH_1, \mathcal{J}_M \cap \mathcal{R}(B)) = mi(A + BH_2, \mathcal{J}_M \cap \mathcal{R}(B)) \quad (2.3.28)$$

where the left and right sides are, respectively, the $(n-1)^{th}$ term of the two sequences of subspaces

$$\begin{cases} S'_0 = \mathcal{J}_M \cap \mathcal{R}(B) \\ \cdots\cdots\cdots \\ S'_K = \mathcal{J}_M \cap \mathcal{R}(B) + (A + BH_1)S'_{K-1} \end{cases}$$

$$\begin{cases} S''_0 = \mathcal{J}_M \cap \mathcal{R}(B) \\ \cdots\cdots\cdots \\ S''_K = \mathcal{J}_M \cap \mathcal{R}(B) + (A + BH_2)S''_{K-1} \end{cases}$$

Under the hypotesis $S'_{i-1} = S''_{i-1}$, it will be shown that $S'_i = S''_i$ and then, being $S'_0 = S''_0$, relationship (2.3.28) will be proved by induction.

First of all, let us remark that all subspaces of the above mentioned sequences are contained in $\mathcal{J}_M$.

Then, let us note that, for every $\underline{x}^* \in S''_{i-1} \subseteq \mathcal{I}_M$

(2.3.29) $(A + BH_2)\underline{x}^* - (A + BH_1)\underline{x}^* \in \mathcal{I}_M$

because $\mathcal{I}_M$ is invariant in both linear transformations $A + BH_1$ and $A + BH_2$.

On the other hand, $\forall \underline{x}^* \in S''_{i-1}$

(2.3.30) $B(H_2 - H_1)\underline{x}^* \in \mathcal{R}(B)$

for the definition of range.

By using the distributivity property, from (2.3.29) and (2.3.30) it immediately follows

(2.3.31) $B(H_2 - H_1)S''_{i-1} \subseteq \mathcal{I}_M \cap \mathcal{R}(B)$.

Now, if we re-write the ith term of the second sequence as

$$S''_i = \mathcal{I}_M \cap \mathcal{R}(B) + (A + BH_1 + B(H_2 - H_1))S''_{i-1} =$$

(2.3.32) $= \mathcal{I}_M \cap \mathcal{R}(B) + (A + BH_1)S''_{i-1} + B(H_2 - H_1)S''_{i-1}$

and if we drop the last term on the right side because of (2.3.31), it turns out

(2.3.33) $S''_i = \mathcal{I}_M \cap \mathcal{R}(B) + (A + BH_1)S''_{i-1} = S'_i$

according to the hypothesis $S''_{i-1} = S'_{i-1}$.

State controllability

2.4. Unconstrained state perfect controllability

The perfect or functional controllability, also called reproducibility, is connected with the possibility of driving the state of the system along any path of the state space, with every time schedule or, in short, along any arbitrary trajectory.

In general, that will be possible only in subspaces of $\mathcal{R}^n$, and since the sum of two subspaces of perfect controllability is still a perfect controllability subspace, one will speak about the greatest perfect controllability subspace which will be called $\mathcal{X}_p$.

Clearly, $\mathcal{X}_p$ <u>is the greatest subspace of $\mathcal{R}^n$ such that at each of its points it is possible to impose any velocity, belonging to $\mathcal{X}_p$ to the system.</u>

Then

$$\mathcal{X}_p \subseteq \mathcal{R}(B) \qquad (2.4.34)$$

because it must be possible to impose every velocity on $\mathcal{X}_p$ at the origin, and

$$\mathcal{X}_p \subseteq A^{-1} * \mathcal{R}(B) \qquad (2.4.35)$$

because it must be possible to impose a null velocity in each point of $\mathcal{X}_p$.

(2.4.34) and (2.4.35) give

$$(2.4.36) \qquad \mathcal{X}_p \subseteq \mathcal{R}(B) \cap A^{-1*}\mathcal{R}(B).$$

Let us now consider the subspace

$$\mathcal{R}(B) \cap A^{-1*}\mathcal{R}(B)$$

and call $\underline{v}$ and $\underline{w}$ two arbitrary points of it.

$$\underline{v} \in \mathcal{R}(B)$$

$$A\underline{w} \in \mathcal{R}(B)$$

and then

$$(2.4.37) \qquad \underline{v} - A\underline{w} \in \mathcal{R}(B).$$

Eq. (2.4.37) means that, for every couple $\underline{v}$ and $\underline{w}$, there exists a control $\underline{u}$ such that

$$(2.4.38) \qquad \underline{v} = A\underline{w} + B\underline{u};$$

or, in other words, after arbitrarily choosing two vectors $\underline{v}$ and $\underline{w}$ in $\mathcal{R}(B) \cap A^{-1*}\mathcal{R}(B)$, one can always find a control $\underline{u}$ such that $\underline{v}$ is the velocity of the system corresponding to the state $\underline{w}$. So, by definition of $\mathcal{X}_p$:

$$(2.4.39) \qquad \mathcal{R}(B) \cap A^{-1*}\mathcal{R}(B) \subseteq \mathcal{X}_p$$

(2.4.39) and (2.4.36) can both be verified only if the equality sign holds and then

$$\mathcal{X}_p = \mathcal{R}(B) \cap A^{-1*}\mathcal{R}(B) \qquad (2.4.40)$$

is the <u>greatest perfect state unconstrained controllability subspace</u>.

2.5. Constrained perfect state controllability

Let us now constrain the problem posed in the previous section in the following way:
given a subspace $W \subseteq \mathcal{R}^n$, find the gratest part of W in which the system can follow any arbitrary trajectory.

Of course, that is possible only at each point of the subspace.

$$\mathcal{X}_{cP} = \mathcal{X}_p \cap W. \qquad (2.5.41)$$

The proof is omitted because it is trivial.

2.6. Output pointwise unconstrained controllability

In transferring the definitions and the characteristic subspaces, previously given, into the output space, the properties of the linear transformation C play a fundamental role.

The case when the output space $\mathcal{R}^s$ is less dimensional than $\mathcal{R}^n$ will be here considered, so that C is a singular matrix. (*)

(+) see note on the following page.

Part Two - Controllability of linear dynamic systems

As is well-known, the null space of C, namely

$$\mathcal{N}(C) = (\mathcal{R}(C^T))^\perp ,$$

is mapped into the origin of $\mathcal{R}^s$ by C, so that a motion of the state in the subspace $\mathcal{N}(C) \subseteq \mathcal{R}^n$ is not visible at the output and the system seems to be in equilibrium at the origin.

On the other hand it has been shown that a motion of the state can take place over an $(A, \mathcal{R}(B))$ controlled invariant; for this reason, in the following, the subspace

$$\mathcal{I}_c = MCI(A, \mathcal{R}(B), \mathcal{N}(C))$$

will take a primary importance.

On the ground of the previous definitions, one can now define the non-constrained reachable set as follows:

The reachable subspace $\mathcal{Y}_R$ is the locus of all the points of the output space reachable starting from the origin, under the hypothesis that the system has been in equilibrium in

---

(+) The case $s = n$, C nonsingular, is trivial. In fact, by means of the substitution $\underline{x} = C^{-1}\underline{y}$, it turns out:

$$\underline{\dot{y}} = CAC^{-1}\underline{y} + CB\underline{u} , \text{ or}$$

$$\underline{\dot{y}} = \hat{A}\underline{y} + \hat{B}\underline{u}$$

and it is possible to discuss directly the properties in the output space as it has been done before in the state space.

Output controllability

the origin for a finite time, before the beginning of the control action.

The reason of this last hypothesis will become clear later on.

Here it will be proved that

$$y_R = C x'_R \qquad (2.6.42)$$

with

$$x'_R = mi(A, \mathcal{J}_c + \mathcal{R}(B)) \qquad (2.6.43)$$

or, writing down the full expression of the $mi(\cdot,\cdot)$

$$\begin{aligned}x'_R &= \mathcal{J}_c + \mathcal{R}(B) + A(\mathcal{J}_c + \mathcal{R}(B)) + \ldots\ldots \\ &= \mathcal{J}_c + mi(A, \mathcal{R}(B)) = \mathcal{J}_c + x_R, \quad (*) \text{ See footnote}\end{aligned} \qquad (2.6.44)$$

because

$$A\mathcal{J}_c \subseteq \mathcal{J}_c + \mathcal{R}(B) , \quad A^2 \mathcal{J}_c \subseteq \mathcal{J}_c + \mathcal{R}(B), \ldots$$

The initial state $\underline{x}_0$ must be in $\mathcal{J}_c$ by virtue of the hypothesis in the definition, and then every input can be

---

(+) Not necessarily a controlled invariant must belong to the reachable set x_R.
In fact, not necessarily a controlled invariant is reachable <u>starting from the origin</u>; and then x'_R may be larger than x_R.

divided into two parts: the first part corresponds to a motion on $\mathcal{J}_c$, the second part corresponds to a motion starting at the origin of $\mathcal{R}^n$ and driving the system in $\mathcal{X}_R$.

The statement is so proved.

Let us now remark that only under the hypothesis of equilibrium in the output origin, the reachable set is a subspace.

In fact, dropping this assumption, let us start a state trajectory from the initial point

$$\underline{x}^* \in \mathcal{N}(C)$$

$$\underline{x}^* \notin \mathcal{J}_c .$$

The reachable set in the states is $\underline{x}^*(t) + \mathcal{X}_R$, where $\underline{x}^*(t)$ is one of the possible trajectories passing through $\underline{x}^*$; <u>no one of these trajectories can belong entirely to $\mathcal{N}(C)$</u>, so at the output it results

$$C \mathcal{X}_R + C \underline{x}^*(t)$$

and the vector $C \underline{x}^*(t)$ does not vanish.

2.7. Output constrained pointwise controllability

Given the subspace $\mathcal{Y}$ of the output space $\mathcal{R}^s$, let us find the greatest part of it reachable from the origin (as an equilibrium point) by means of trajectories completely belonging to it.

Output controllability

The state trajectory must be in

$$x = C^{-1*}y = \tilde{C}^{-1}(y \cap \mathcal{R}(C)) + \mathcal{N}(C) \qquad (2.7.45)$$

and, as a state trajectory can stay only over a controlled invariant, let us compute

$$\mathcal{J} = MCI(A, \mathcal{R}(B), C^{-1*}y) . \qquad (2.7.46)$$

The reachable part of $\mathcal{J}$ starting from the state origin is

$$\mathcal{X}' = mi(A + BH, \mathcal{J} \cap \mathcal{R}(B)) \qquad (2.7.47)$$

where H is one of the matrices such that

$$(A + BH)\mathcal{J} \subseteq \mathcal{J}.$$

Then the part of $\mathcal{Y}$ reachable by trajectories on it, is

$$y' = C\mathcal{X}' \subseteq \mathcal{Y} \qquad (2.7.48)$$

Again, if the system must be in equilibrium in $y = 0$ before the control action begins, one has to start from a point $\underline{x} \in \mathcal{J}_c$ of the state space $(\mathcal{J}_c = MCI(A, \mathcal{R}(B), \mathcal{N}(C)) \subseteq \mathcal{J})$, and again every arbitrary law of control $\underline{u}(t)$ can be decomposed in a control $\underline{u}_1(t)$ which gives a trajectory on $\mathcal{J}_c$, plus an arbitrary control $\underline{u}_2(t)$ which spans the complete $\mathcal{R}(B)$.

2.8. General considerations on the perfect output controllability

In transferring into the output space the concept of perfect controllability, a very interesting situation arises: the extensions of the characteristic subspaces depend on the class of functions to which the system trajectory belongs.

Let us be more explicit by means of a simple example:
Consider the system

$$\dot{x}_1 = -x_1 + u_1 \qquad y_1 = -x_1$$
$$\dot{x}_2 = x_1 + x_3 \qquad y_2 = x_2$$
$$\dot{x}_3 = -x_2 + x_2$$

with a threedimensional state space, a twodimensional output space, and characteristic matrices

$$A = \begin{bmatrix} -1 & 0 & 0 \\ 1 & 0 & 1 \\ 0 & 1 & 1 \end{bmatrix}, \quad B = \begin{bmatrix} 1 & 0 \\ 0 & 0 \\ 0 & 1 \end{bmatrix}, \quad C = \begin{bmatrix} -1 & 0 & 0 \\ 0 & 1 & 0 \end{bmatrix}.$$

$\mathcal{R}(B)$ is the plane (x_1, x_3), $\mathcal{N}(C)$ is the x_3 axis, and $\mathcal{R}(C^T)$ is the (x_1, x_2) plane. It is very easy to verify that the gratest state perfect controllability subspace is the straight line

$$(2.8.49) \quad \mathcal{X}_p = \mathcal{L} = \left\{ \underline{x} : \underline{x} = \begin{vmatrix} -1 \\ 0 \\ 1 \end{vmatrix} \alpha, \ \alpha \text{ real, arb.} \right\}$$

Output controllability

In fact, starting at the origin, x_2 remains always equal to zero if $\dot{x}_2 = 0$, and this is true (see the second state equation) if the state motion takes place over $\mathcal{L}$. To this purpose the second component of the control in the third state equation, must be chosen properly.

At this point, the choice of u_1, and then the choice of the time schedule for the motion on $\mathcal{L}$, is still free.

Since $\mathcal{X}_p = \mathcal{L}$ is mapped by C into the first axis of the output space, it seems that the only output perfect controllability subspace is

$$C\mathcal{X}_p = \left\{ \underline{y} : \underline{y} = \begin{vmatrix} 1 \\ 0 \end{vmatrix} \beta, \ \beta \ \text{real, arb.} \right\}. \quad (2.8.50)$$

But, by deriving the system equations, and by making some substitutions, one gets:

$$\begin{aligned}\ddot{y}_1 &= x_1 - u_1 - \dot{u}_1 \\ \ddot{y}_2 &= -x_1 - x_2 + u_1 + u_2,\end{aligned} \quad (2.8.51)$$

from which it clearly appears that it is possible to impose arbitrarily the values of the second derivatives of the output trajectories in the full output space.

Concluding, the output perfect controllability subspace with respect to the first derivatives is the y_1 axis; with respect to the second derivatives is the (y_1, y_2) plane.

In general it will be shown that the smoother is

the trajectory on which one wants to drive the system output, the larger is the corresponding characteristic subspace.

2.9. Unconstrained perfect output controllability

Let us consider the equation

$$(2.9.52) \qquad \underline{\dot{y}} = CA\underline{x} + CB\underline{u} ,$$

obtained by taking the time derivative of the state-output relationship, $\underline{y} = C\underline{x}$, and by substituting $\underline{\dot{x}} = A\underline{x} + B\underline{u}$.

Matrix CB maps the control space $\mathcal{R}^m$, into the output space $\mathcal{R}^s$, then (see a.1, a.2)

$$(2.9.53) \qquad \mathcal{N}(CB) + \mathcal{R}(B^T C^T) = \mathcal{R}^m ,$$

and then every control can be decomposed as follows:

$$\underline{u} = \underline{u}_N + \underline{u}_R , \quad \underline{u}_N \in \mathcal{N}(CB) , \quad \underline{u}_R \in \mathcal{R}(B^T C^T) .$$

Let P_N and P_R be projection matrices such that

$$\underline{u}_N = P_N \underline{u} , \quad \underline{u}_R = P_R \underline{u} .$$

P_N clearly projects $\mathcal{R}^m$ into $\mathcal{N}(CB)$, and then

$$(2.9.54) \qquad \mathcal{R}(P_N) = \mathcal{N}(CB) ,$$

P_R projects $\mathcal{R}^m$ into $\mathcal{R}(B^T C^T)$ and then

$$(2.9.55) \qquad \mathcal{R}(P_R) = \mathcal{R}(B^T C^T) .$$

Output controllability

Decomposing the control as has been shown, (2.9.52) becomes

$$\dot{\underline{y}} = CA\underline{x} + CBP_R\underline{u} \;, \qquad (2.9.56)$$

because $CBP_N\underline{u}$ clearly vanishes.

Projection P_R does not affect the transformation CB (see Appendix of Part One), thus, ranging $\underline{u}$ in $\mathcal{R}^m$, $CBP_R\underline{u}$ ranges in the full

$$\mathcal{R}(CB) = C\,\mathcal{R}(B) \;;$$

Therefore it is possible to choose the first derivative of the output in the subspace

$$\mathcal{Y}_o = CS_o = C\,\mathcal{R}(B) \;. \qquad (2.9.57)$$

Taking the time derivative of (2.9.56) and substituting, it results

$$\ddot{\underline{y}} = CA^2\underline{x} + CBP_R\dot{\underline{u}} + CABP_N\underline{u} + CABP_R\underline{u} \;. \qquad (2.9.58)$$

Since the term $CABP_N\underline{u}$ is completely free, the second derivative of $\underline{y}$ can be arbitrarily chosen in

$$CAB\,\mathcal{R}(P_N) \;.$$

Using (2.9.54), such a subspace can be written as

$$CAB\,\mathcal{R}(P_N) = CA(\mathcal{R}(B) \cap \mathcal{N}(C)) \;. \qquad (2.9.59)$$

Then the choice of the first and the second derivatives is completely free in the subspace.

(2.9.60) $\quad y_1 = CS_1 = C(\mathcal{R}(B) + A(S_0 \cap \mathcal{N}(C)))$.

The iteration of this procedure gives the sequence of subspaces

(2.9.61) $\quad S_0 = \mathcal{R}(B), \; S_1 = S_0 + A(S_0 \cap \mathcal{N}(C)), \ldots$

$\quad \ldots, S_k = S_{k-1} + A(S_{k-1} \cap \mathcal{N}(C))$.

and it ends with the greatest subspace where it is possible to control the nth derivatives:

(2.9.62) $\quad y_n = CS_{n-1} = C\,mci(A, \mathcal{N}(C), \mathcal{R}(B))$.

2.10. Constrained perfect output controllability

Given a subspace $\mathcal{Y}$ of the output space $\mathcal{R}^s$, let us find the greatest part of $\mathcal{Y}$ in which it is possible to choose arbitrarily the first derivative of the trajectory.

In order to solve the problem, look for a subspace S of the state space such that:

a) S is a locus of state trajectories and then an $(A, \mathcal{R}(B))$ controlled invariant.
b) $S \subseteq S_0 = C^{-1*}\mathcal{Y}$
c) $S \subseteq S \cap \mathcal{R}(B) + \mathcal{N}(C)$

Output controllability

The last condition means that S is mapped into the output by matrix C as its intersection with $\mathcal{R}(B)$, or in other words, the set of all possible arbitrary velocities on S mapped by C into the output, covers CS completely.

Then compute

$$S^* = MCI(A, \mathcal{R}(B), S_0 \cap \mathcal{R}(B) + \mathcal{N}(C)). \quad (2.10.63)$$

If $S^* = S_0$, S^* satisfies conditions a), b) and c) and it is the solution of the posed problem.

If it is not, call it S_1 and compute

$$S_2 = MCI(A, \mathcal{R}(B), S_1 \cap \mathcal{R}(B) + \mathcal{N}(C)),$$

and so on; in general

$$S_k = MCI(A, \mathcal{R}(B), S_{k-1} \cap \mathcal{R}(B) + \mathcal{N}(C)). \quad (2.10.64)$$

When for some r

$$S_r = S_{r-1}, \quad (2.10.65)$$

S_r satisfies conditions a), b) and c).

As sequence (2.10.64) at most stops in $(n-1)$ steps, one can always say that

$$S_{n-1} = S_{n-1}^{(1)}$$

is the unknown subspace, and

(2.10.66) $$y^{(1)} = C S_{n-1}^{(1)},$$

is the greatest part of $\mathcal{Y}$ where the trajectory is perfectly controllable with respect to the first derivatives.

Let us now carry out the same reasoning for the second derivatives.

Look for a subspace of $\mathcal{R}^n$ such that:

a) $S^{(2)}$ is a controlled invariant
b) $S^{(2)}$ is contained in $S_0 = C^{-1*}\mathcal{Y}$
c) $S^{(2)} \subseteq S^{(2)} \cap Z_1 + \mathcal{N}(C)$

Condition c) has the same meaning previously discussed, with respect to the new set Z_1 of the allowable variations of the second derivatives; its expression is

(2.10.67) $$Z_1 = \mathcal{R}(B) + A(S_0 \cap \mathcal{R}(B) \cap \mathcal{N}(C)).$$

The second term of the right side member is the set of all the possible variations of the second derivatives due to a direct manipulations of the controls belonging to $S_0 \cap \mathcal{R}(B)$ and invisible at the output.

Again compute

$$S^* = MCI(A, \mathcal{R}(B), S_0 \cap Z_1 + \mathcal{N}(C)) \qquad (2.10.68)$$

if $S^* = S_0$, the full S_0 satisfies conditions a), b) and c).

If it is not, recompute the MCI, introducing a new restriction also on the set Z_1.

To this purpose it is useful to write down the double sequence of subspaces:

S_0

$$Z_{0,1} = \mathcal{R}(B)$$

$$Z_{1,1} = \mathcal{R}(B) + A(S_0 \cap Z_{0,1} \cap \mathcal{N}(C))$$

$$S_1 = MCI(A, \mathcal{R}(B), S_0 \cap Z_{1,1} + \mathcal{N}(C))$$

$$Z_{0,2} = \mathcal{R}(B)$$

$$Z_{1,2} = \mathcal{R}(B) + A(S_1 \cap Z_{0,2} \cap \mathcal{N}(C))$$

$$S_2 = MCI(A, \mathcal{R}(B), S_1 \cap Z_{1,2} + \mathcal{N}(C))$$

$$Z_{0,3} = \mathcal{R}(B)$$

$$Z_{1,3} = \ldots\ldots$$

The first index of the right side sequences stops at 1, because the problem considered here concerns the second derivatives; in the general case of kth-order derivatives, it stops at $k-1$.

Now, as the left side sequence at most stops in $(n-1)$ steps, one can always conclude that

$$S^{(2)} = S_{n-1} \quad \text{and} \quad y^{(2)} = CS^{(2)}.$$

In the case of controllability with respect to the kth derivatives,

$$S^{(k)} = S_{n-1} \quad \text{and} \quad y^{(k)} = CS^{(k)},$$

where S_{n-1} is the last term of the left side sequence, extending up to the $(k-1)^{th}$ term of the right side sequences.

References

[1] Basile, G. and Marro, G., "On the Observability of Linear, Time-Invariant Systems with Unknown Inputs" Journal of Optimization Theory and Applications, Vol. 3, N. 6, June 1969.

[2] Kalman, R.E., "On the General Theory of Control Systems" Proocedings of the First IFAC Congress, Vol. 1, Butterworths, London, 1961.

[3] Kreindler, E. and Sarackik, P.E., "On the Concepts of Controllability and Observability in Linear Systems", IEEE Transactions on Automatic Control, Vol. AC-9, N. 2, 1964.

[4] Weiss, L., "The Concepts of Differential Controllability and Differential Observability", Journal of Mathematical Analysis and Applications, Vol. 10, N. 2, 1965.

[5] Basile, G. and Marro, G. "On the Perfect Output Controllability of Linear Dynamic Systems" Ricerche di Automatica, Vol. 1, N. 2, Marzo 1971.

[6] Basile, G. and Marro, G., "A State Approach to Non-interacting Controls" Ricerche di Automatica, Vol. 1, N. 1, Settembre 1970.

[7] Basile, G. and Marro, G., "On the Multi-level Functional Output Controllability of Linear Systems" Int. 1 IEEE Conference, Oaxtepec Morelos, Mexico, Gennaio 1971.

Contents

	Page
Foreword	3
Introduction	5
Part One – Generalization of the concept of invariance	6
1.1 The simple invariance	6
1.2 The controlled invariance	7
1.3 The conditioned invariance	8
1.4 A fundamental duality property	8
1.5 Computational procedures for the controlled and conditioned invariants	11
Appendix – The pseudoinverse of a singular matrix	16
References	18
Part Two – Controllability of linear dynamic systems	19
2.1 Preliminary definitions	19
2.2 Unconstrained state pointwise controllability	20
2.3 Constrained state pointwise controllability	23
2.4 Unconstrained state perfect controllability	33
2.5 Constrained perfect state controllability	35
2.6 Output pointwise unconstrained controllability	35
2.7 Output constrained pointwise controllability	38
2.8 General considerations on the perfect output controllability	40
2.9 Unconstrained perfect output controllability	42
2.10 Constrained perfect output controllability	44
References	49

MIX
Papier aus verantwortungsvollen Quellen
Paper from responsible sources
FSC® C105338

If you have any concerns about our products,
you can contact us on
ProductSafety@springernature.com

In case Publisher is established outside the EU,
the EU authorized representative is:
**Springer Nature Customer Service Center GmbH
Europaplatz 3, 69115 Heidelberg, Germany**

Printed by Libri Plureos GmbH
in Hamburg, Germany